NOV

A WORLD OF RECIPES

Christmas Foods

REVISED AND UPDATED

Jenny Vaughan and Penny Beauchamp

Heinemann Library
Chicago, Illinois

www.heinemannraintree.com
Visit our website to find out
more information about
Heinemann-Raintree books.

To order:

☎ Phone 888-454-2279

▣ Visit www.heinemannraintree.com
to browse our catalog and order online.

© 2004, 2009 Heinemann Library
an imprint of Capstone Global Library, LLC
Chicago, Illinois

Edited by David Andrews and Diyan Leake
Designed by Richard Parker
Illustrated by Nicholas Beresford-Davis
Picture research by Mica Brancic
Printed and bound in China by Leo Paper Products Ltd

13 12 11 10 09
10 9 8 7 6 5 4 3 2 1

New ISBNs: 978-1-4329-2237-5

**The Library of Congress has cataloged the first edition
as follows:**
Vaughn, Jenny.
    Christmas foods/Jenny Vaughn and Penny Beauchamp
    p. cm. -- (A world of recipes)
    Includes bibliographical references and index.
    Summary: Includes easy to read Christmas recipes from
different cultures around the world.
    ISBN 978-1-4034-4697-8 (HC) 978-1-4034-6011-0
1.   Christmas cookery—Juvenile literature. 2. Cookery,
International—Juvenile literature. 3. [1. Christmas cookery.
2. Cookery, International.] I. Beauchamp, Penny. II. Title.
TX739.2.C45V38 2004
641.5'686—dc22   20030018012

Acknowledgments

The author and publishers are grateful to the following for
permission to reproduce copyright material: © Capstone
Global Library Ltd/MM Studios pp. **32, 33**; Corbis p. **4** (©
Atlantide Phototravel/Guido Cozzi); Photolibrary Group pp.
6 (Food Collection), **7** (SGM SGM); Private Collection p. **5**
(Bridgeman Art Library); Steve Lee pp. **24, 25, 30, 34–43**;
Terry Benson pp. **10–23, 26–29.**

Cover photograph of mince pies reproduced with permission
of Corbis (moodboard).

Every effort has been made to contact copyright holders of
any material reproduced in this book. Any omissions will
be rectified in subsequent printings if notice is given to the
publisher.

All the Internet addresses (URLs) given in this book were valid
at the time of going to press. However, due to the dynamic
nature of the Internet, some addresses may have changed, or
sites may have changed or ceased to exist since publication.
While the author and Publishers regret any inconvenience this
may cause readers, no responsibility for any such changes can
be accepted by either the author or the Publishers.

Contents

Some words are shown in bold, **like this**. You can find out what they mean by looking in the glossary.

Christmas

Christmas is a holiday celebrated in countries all over the world. This holiday honors the birth of Jesus Christ, the founder of the Christian religion. The word *Christmas* was first used in England in 1050.

↑ This choir is giving a Christmas concert in Sweden.

Mid-winter celebrations

Mid-winter celebrations were held long before the birth of Jesus. In ancient Rome, the feast of Saturnalia honored the god of agriculture. A Yule log was burned in Scandinavia to celebrate the return of the sun.

The Roman Catholic Church chose mid-winter as a time to honor the birth of Jesus. As Christianity spread, more people celebrated Christmas instead of the older feasts.

The original story of Christmas comes from the Bible. According to tradition, Jesus was born in a stable when his mother Mary and her husband, Joseph, were traveling through the town of Bethlehem. He was visited by three kings, who brought gifts. Angels announced his birth to the shepherds in the field nearby.

Christmas traditions

One of the most popular symbols of Christmas is Saint Nicholas, also known as Santa Claus. A bishop named Nicholas lived in Turkey during the 4th century. He was a generous man who gave gifts to children. After his death, it was believed he rode through the sky on a white horse. The Dutch name for him, Sinter Klaas, was brought to the United States by Dutch settlers and changed into Santa Claus.

You might hang up a stocking for Santa Claus to fill with gifts. In the Netherlands, children leave a wooden shoe with straw in it for his horse! Children in Puerto Rico place greenery in boxes beneath their beds for the camels of the Three Kings.

In Italy, children do not wait for Santa Claus on Christmas Eve. Instead, they look forward to a good witch on a broom on the Eve of Epiphany (January 5).

↑ This is a Christmas card from England in the 19th century.

The Christmas tree was a symbol of rebirth in 17th-century Germany. This was because it stayed green all winter, when other trees were bare. Decorations may have been hung on trees as early as the 15th century. The custom spread to England in 1841, when the German Prince Albert gave a tree to his English wife, Queen Victoria.

Christmas Food

Poultry, or birds that are raised to be eaten, is traditional at Christmas dinner in many countries. In England in the Middle Ages, swans and peacocks were served.

Geese have also been used for centuries to celebrate important events. People in Europe ate goose at mid-winter festivals. Goose, served with red cabbage, remains a popular Christmas dish in Scandinavia. In France, goose might be served stuffed with chestnuts.

↑ Roast goose is a popular Christmas dish.

In the United States and the United Kingdom, turkey makes a popular Christmas meal. In Ethiopia, you might eat spicy chicken stew scooped up with flat bread.

Fish is also traditionally served in some countries. **Baked** carp is often served in Germany and Poland.

Sweet treats

Christmas pudding is a traditional English dessert that was first served at Christmas in the 18th century. Small coins were baked in the pudding. It was thought that whoever found a coin in his or her serving would be wealthy in the coming year.

In Denmark, rice pudding is placed outside on Christmas Eve for a playful elf. People eat the pudding, too. It is made with an almond in it that is said to be magic.

The Three Kings cake, in France, contains a bean. Whoever finds the bean in his or her serving is king or queen for the day.

Yule logs were once burned in countries ranging from Scandinavia to Greece. Today, people often do not have fireplaces to burn a log. Many people eat a log instead—a log of cake! This tradition began in France. The thin cake is rolled up to look like a log. It is often iced in chocolate and decorated with holly leaves.

Christmas cookies are another sweet treat. Ingredients such as spices, nuts, and dried fruit were brought to Europe in the Middle Ages. Bakers soon began using them. Dutch and German treats, including gingerbread men, often include ginger. Norwegian bakers made lemon wafers. Sugar cookie recipes were first used in England. Today, you can bake Christmas cookies in many shapes, including bells, trees, and even camels!

↑ Tempting holiday foods are sold at Christmas markets. This one is in France.

Ingredients

honey

candied cherries

cloves

ground cinnamon

flaked almonds

ground almonds

candied peel

stock cube

cinnamon

nutmeg

Preserved fruit

Many Christmas recipes include cherries that have been preserved in sugar, and lemon and orange peel treated in the same way. You can buy **candied** cherries and other candied fruit, such as mixed peel, from supermarkets. The tradition of using preserved fruit began before people had refrigerators, when it was hard to find fresh food in the middle of winter.

Spices

Christmas foods often contain spices such as nutmeg, cinnamon, or cloves. Spices were very popular in the past because food was often eaten when it was rather old. The strong flavor of the spices disguised the taste of the food, even if it was going bad. Today, we know that it is dangerous to eat bad food, but the tradition of using spices in many types of winter food has lived on.

Honey

Honey is used to sweeten many classic Christmas recipes. Some recipes might ask you to heat honey or sugar. It is important to have an adult with you when you do this because heated honey or sugar can become very hot.

Stock

Cooks always used to make tasty stock by **boiling** up bones such as chicken bones for hours and hours. The bones gave the water a rich flavor, and this stock could be used as a base for soups and stews. Today, you can buy stock cubes and make instant stock by **dissolving** them in water. There are meat, fish, or vegetable stock cubes. This makes the cooking process much easier.

Nuts

Many Christmas recipes include nuts. Almonds are very popular, and they can be bought ready-**chopped**, **toasted**, flaked, or ground. Other popular nuts include pecans, cashews, and pistachios. If you need to toast nuts yourself, be careful, as they burn very easily. Keep a close eye on them as they are toasting in the oven.

Some people are allergic to nuts. This means that it is very dangerous for them to eat food with even the tiniest trace of nuts in it. Always check that it is okay for your guests to eat nuts. Never serve food with nuts in it to anyone with a nut allergy.

Before You Start

Which recipe should I try?

The recipes you choose to make depend on many things. Some recipes make a good main course, while others are better as starters. Some are easy, while others are more difficult.

The top right-hand page of each recipe has information that can help you. It tells you how long each recipe will take and how many people it serves. You can multiply or divide the quantities if you want to cook for more or fewer people. This section also shows how difficult each dish is to make: the recipes are easy (*), medium (**), or difficult (***) to cook.

This symbol is sign of a dangerous step in a recipe. For these steps, be extra careful or ask an adult to help.

Kitchen rules

There are a few basic rules you should always follow when you cook:

- Ask an adult if you can use the kitchen.
- Wash your hands before you start.
- Wear an apron to protect your clothes. Tie back long hair.
- Be very careful when using sharp knives.
- Never leave pan handles sticking out—it could be dangerous if you bump into them.
- Always wear oven mits to lift things in and out of the oven.
- Wash fruits and vegetables before you use them.

Quantities and measurements

Ingredients for recipes can be measured in two different ways. Imperial measurements use cups, pounds, ounces, and fluid ounces. Metric measurements use grams, liters, and milliliters. In the recipes in this book you will see the following abbreviations:

tbsp = tablespoons

tsp = teaspoons

lbs = pounds

oz. = ounces

g = grams

in. = inches

cm = centimeters

ml = milliliters

Utensils

To cook the recipes in this book, you will need these utensils, as well as kitchen essentials, such as spoons, plates, and bowls.

- Baking sheet, preferably nonstick
- 8-in. (20-cm) cake pan
- Chopping board
- Cooling rack
- Food processor or blender
- Grater
- Heavy frying pan with a lid
- Kitchen scale
- Large nonstick saucepan
- Measuring cup (for liquids)
- Measuring cups (for dry ingredients) and measuring spoons
- Muffin pan
- **Ovenproof** dish
- **Parchment paper**
- Pastry brush (for glazing)
- Potato masher
- Rolling pin and board
- Set of pastry cutters
- Sharp knife
- Sieve or **colander**
- Skewer
- Spatula
- Wax paper
- Whisk

Shrimp Snacks (Philippines)

The Philippines has a hot, **tropical** climate. The Christmas meal is usually a combination of light and tasty snacks. These shrimp fritters are called ukoy.

What you need

3.5 oz. shelled, cooked shrimp
½ cup all-purpose flour
1 tsp baking powder
A pinch of salt
1 small clove of garlic
1 green onion
1 egg
A pinch of white pepper
¼ cup water
Vegetable oil

What you do

1. **Chop** the shrimp up into small pieces.

2. Mix the flour, baking powder, and salt together in a bowl.

3. Crush the clove of garlic and chop the green onion. Then **beat** the egg and mix it with the garlic and onion. **Season** with pepper.

4. Add the water to the egg and onion, then beat this mixture into the flour. It should form a thick, creamy **batter**. If not, add more water, a little at a time, until it forms a batter.

5. Add the shrimp and mix them in well.

6. Pour enough vegetable oil into a heavy frying pan to cover it to a depth of about 1/4 in. (½ cm). Turn the heat up under the pan until it is hot enough to make a drop of your batter sizzle. Be very careful, as the oil may spatter.

7 Drop a few spoonfuls of the batter into the pan. Cook for about two minutes and then, very carefully, turn the ukoy over with a spatula. They should be brown on one side. Cook the other side for about two more minutes, until it is brown as well.

8 Take the ukoy out of the pan with the spatula and drain them on paper towels. Keep them somewhere warm.

SEASONING WITH SOY

Try **sprinkling** a little soy sauce over the ukoy.
Most people enjoy them even more this way.

Festive Mushroom Soup (Poland)

In Poland, the most important Christmas meal is eaten on Christmas Eve, before Midnight Mass, the special communion service that marks the beginning of Christmas Day. It is traditional not to eat meat at this meal. This simple vegetarian soup forms one of several courses.

What you need

- 3½ cups brown, flat-cap mushrooms
- 1 large onion
- 1 tbsp vegetable oil
- 4 cups water
- 2 vegetable stock cubes
- Juice of ½ lemon
- ½ cup fresh sour cream
- 2 slices of white or brown bread
- 1 tbsp parsley, chopped

What you do

1 **Chop** the mushrooms and the onion.

2 Heat the oil in a pan and **fry** them for about five minutes, until the onion is **translucent** and the mushrooms are cooked.

3 Bring 4 cups (1 liter) of water to a **boil** in a saucepan and add the stock cubes. Stir until they have **dissolved**. They will dissolve better if you crumble them as you are adding them to the water.

4 Add the lemon juice and the cooked onion and mushrooms to the vegetable stock.

5 Let the soup **simmer** for about 15 minutes.

6 Take the soup off the heat and add the sour cream, stirring very quickly.

7 Cut the crusts off the bread, **broil** it on both sides, and then cut it into little cubes.

8 Serve the soup in bowls, **sprinkling** a few cubes of bread and some fresh, chopped parsley on top.

Chicken and Meatball Soup (Palestine)

Although most people in Palestine are Muslims, there are many Arab Christians living there, too. This recipe is based on a soup that a Palestinian writer remembers her mother making on Christmas morning.

What you need

4 cups water
2 chicken stock cubes
½ onion
½ tsp **grated** nutmeg
1 tsp cinnamon
9 oz. ground lamb
1 tbsp vegetable oil
¼ cup long-grain rice
1 tbsp tomato paste
1 tbsp fresh parsley, chopped

What you do

1. Make the stock by **boiling** the water in a pan and crumbling the stock cubes into it. Turn the heat off and stir the stock cubes into the water until they have **dissolved** completely.

2. **Chop** the onion into very fine strips.

3. Mix the onions, spices, and lamb together.

4. Using your hands, make the lamb mixture into small meatballs, each one a little bigger than a marble. Wash your hands.

5. Heat the oil in a pan, then **fry** the meatballs until they are cooked through and nicely browned on the outside.

6 Reheat the stock until it is boiling, then turn down the heat so that it **simmers** gently. Add the rice, the tomato **paste**, and the meatballs.

7 Let the soup simmer for about 30 minutes, until the rice is cooked all the way through.

8 Serve the soup in bowls, with chopped parsley **sprinkled** over it.

Niños Envueltos (Argentina)

The name of this recipe means "babies in blankets," because that is what it is supposed to look like! It is a good reminder of what Christmas is all about—the birth of baby Jesus.

What you need

½ cup frozen leaf spinach

2 x 4-oz. rump or sirloin steaks

Salt and pepper

1 hard-boiled egg

5 oz. cooked ham

1 tbsp butter

4 sprigs rosemary and some string

1 tbsp all-purpose flour

1 tbsp vegetable oil

8-oz. canned chopped tomatoes

What you do

1 Allow the frozen spinach to **thaw**, and then **chop** it up roughly.

2 Put the spinach in a **colander** and, using a spoon, press it hard so that as much water as possible is squeezed out.

3 **Season** the meat with salt and pepper.

4 Chop up the hard-boiled egg and the ham into very small pieces.

5 Mix the spinach, butter, ham, and egg together. Spoon the mixture onto the pieces of steak.

6 Roll up the pieces of steak. Tie them up and spear each of them with two sprigs of rosemary.

7 **Sprinkle** the flour onto a dish and roll the bundles of meat in it until they are entirely coated.

 8 Heat the oil in a heavy pan and **fry** the pieces of meat for one or two minutes, turning them over at least once. When they are brown all over, add the tomatoes.

9 Put a lid on the pan and cook it over low heat for about 20 minutes. Check occasionally to see if it is getting too dry. If it is, add a little water to moisten.

10 Serve one "baby" roll for each person, with potatoes and a green salad.

Savory Rice (Brazil)

This tasty rice recipe is popular on any special occasion in Brazil, including Christmas. Try it with turkey leftovers the day after Christmas, or cook it to go with another South American dish—the Argentinian *niños envueltos* on pages 18–19.

What you need

1 small onion
½ chicken stock cube
1½ cups water
½ tbsp olive oil
1 cup long-grain rice
2 tbsp **chopped**,
   canned tomatoes
Salt

What you do

1 **Slice** the onion thinly.

2 Crumble the stock cube into the water in a saucepan, then bring to a **boil**.

3 Warm the oil in a large saucepan, tipping the pan to coat the base evenly. Add the onion and **fry** it for five minutes, or until it is **translucent** but not yet brown.

4 Pour in the rice and stir for three minutes, until all the grains are coated with the oil. (Do not let the rice brown.)

5 Add the stock to the rice. Add the tomatoes and **season** with salt. Return the mixture to a boil, stirring it occasionally.

6 **Cover** the saucepan and turn the heat down low so that the rice is just **simmering**.

7 Cook for 20 minutes or until the rice has **absorbed** all the liquid in the pan.

8 If the rice seems to be drying out, add a little more water and stir well. If it seems to be cooked before 20 minutes, stop heating or it will get mushy and sticky.

9 Pile the rice onto warm plates and serve immediately.

Jansson's Temptation (Sweden)

In Scandinavia, winters are long, dark, and cold. This warming potato dish is traditionally eaten around Christmastime. Anchovies are very small, salty fish that add real flavor to the dish. You can make the recipe without the anchovies, but then you will probably want to add salt along with the pepper.

What you need

1 lb **waxy potatoes**
1 onion
2 tbsp butter
8 anchovies, chopped (optional)
Black pepper
1 cup whipping cream
1 tbsp chopped parsley

What you do

1 **Preheat** the oven to 325°F (160°C).

2 **Peel** the potatoes and onion and **slice** them all thinly.

3 Rub some butter on the inside of an **ovenproof** dish. Use a round dish, about 8 in. (20 cm) across. Set the remaining butter aside.

4 Place a layer of potatoes in the dish, followed by a layer of onions and a few anchovies. Add another layer of potatoes, continuing until all the potatoes, onions, and anchovies are used up. End with a layer of potatoes.

5 Grind a little black pepper over the potatoes. You will only need to add salt if you have not used anchovies. Now pour the cream over the potatoes.

6 Cut the rest of the butter up into small pieces, each about the size of a pea, and scatter these over the potatoes. **Cover** the dish with wax paper.

7 **Bake** it for about 45 minutes. Remove the paper and turn the heat up to 350°F (180°C) and bake for another 30 minutes, until the top is golden and the potatoes are cooked through.

8 **Sprinkle** with **chopped** parsley just before serving.

Mince Pies (England)

Mince pies are served throughout the Christmas season in England. They are little pies filled with a fruit mixture called mincemeat.

What you need

2 cups cooking apples
2 tbsp water
1 tbsp granulated sugar
Juice of 1 orange
3 cups dried, mixed fruit
10 tbsp butter
1 cup brown sugar
5 tbsp mixed **candied** peel
1/3 cup **chopped** almonds
1/3 tsp cinnamon
1/3 tsp nutmeg
1/3 tsp allspice
1 tsp molasses
2 tbsp all-purpose flour
Ready-made pie pastry **dough**
A little milk
1 tsp powdered sugar

What you do

 **1** **Peel** and core the apples, and then **grate** them.

 **2** Put the apples in a pan with the water and all the other ingredients except for the flour, pastry, milk, and powdered sugar. **Simmer** until the apples are soft.

3 Put the cooked mixture in a bowl. **Cover** the bowl and put it in the refrigerator. You can use it after two hours, but it tastes better after three to four days.

4 **Preheat** the oven to 400°F (200°C).

5 **Grease** a muffin pan. **Sprinkle** the flour onto a board, and then roll the pastry out as thinly as possible. Cut 12 circles and place them in a greased muffin pan.

6 Fill each opening with mincemeat to the level of the edges of the pastry.

7 Gather up the remains of the pastry. Press it into a ball, then roll it out and cut lids from it, using a slightly smaller cutter. Dampen the edge of each lid with water before pressing it lightly over the filling.

8 Brush each mince pie with milk and then make a small slit in the lid with the point of a knife.

9 **Bake** the mince pies for about 25 minutes, or until they are light golden brown. Sprinkle with sugar.

Ghryba Shortbread (Egypt)

Christians in Egypt celebrate Christmas with many different kinds of cakes and pastries, including these shortbreads. Their Muslim neighbors use the same recipe to celebrate the end of their annual month of fasting, which is called Ramadan.

What you need

- 1 cup butter
- ½ cup powdered sugar
- 1½ cups all-purpose flour
- 12–15 **peeled**, halved almonds or pine nuts

What you do

1 **Preheat** the oven to 350°F (180°C).

 2 Melt the butter gently in a medium, nonstick pan. Turn off the heat.

3 Add the powdered sugar to the melted butter and mix in well.

4 Using a wooden spoon, add the flour a little at a time, stirring well. Keep adding flour until you have a soft **dough**.

5 By now your dough will be cool enough to handle. Roll it into balls of about the size as a marble.

6 Flatten the balls of dough out to make small rounds. If the baking sheet is not nonstick, line it with **parchment paper**, and then put the rounds on the sheet.

7 Press an almond or pine nut into the center of each dough round.

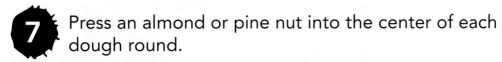

8 **Bake** the dough rounds for about 8 to 10 minutes, until the nuts are browned but the cookies are still a pale cream color. Do not let them turn brown.

9 **Cool** the cookies on a cooling rack until they are hard and cool enough to eat.

Melomakarona (Greece)

The most important festival of the year in Greece is Easter, but this does not mean that Christmas goes by unnoticed. There are always plenty of good things to eat on Christmas Day—such as these little cakes soaked in honey.

What you need

½ cup olive oil

½ cup granulated sugar

1½ tbsp freshly
squeezed orange juice

3/4 cup honey

2 cups all-purpose flour

¼ tsp allspice

¼ tsp nutmeg

½ tsp **grated**
orange peel

1 tsp baking powder

1 tbsp powdered sugar
(optional)

¼ tsp ground
cinnamon

Walnuts, **chopped**
(optional)

What you do

1 **Preheat** the oven to 350°F (180°C).

2 **Beat** together the oil, 2 tbsp of the sugar, the orange juice, and a third of the honey.

3 Mix the flour, cinammon, nutmeg, allspice, orange peel, and baking powder together, and add it to the oil and sugar mixture.

4 Mix all these ingredients together in a bowl to form a soft **dough**.

5 Divide the dough into four pieces and roll them between your hands to make hotdog shapes about 1 in. wide. Cut each hotdog shape into sections about 2 in. long.

  **6** Place the shapes on a baking sheet. If the sheet is not nonstick, line it with **parchment paper**. **Bake** for about 30 minutes.

7 Put the remaining honey in a small, nonstick pan and add the remaining granulated sugar. Heat gently until **dissolved**, and then let the mixture **boil** for about five minutes.

 8 When you take the cakes out of the oven, put them in a shallow dish. Pour the warm **syrup** over them. Leave them for five minutes.

 9 Using a spatula, put the cakes on a serving plate and **sprinkle** them with powdered sugar mixed with ground cinnamon. You can also scatter some walnuts over the cakes if you like.

Stollen (Austria)

Stollen is a Christmas bread. It is meant to look like a baby wrapped in old-fashioned swaddling clothes, to remind people of Jesus as a baby.

What you need

Grated peel and juice of a lemon

½ cup candied peel

1 cup diced, mixed dried fruit

1 tsp nutmeg

1 cup orange juice

3½ cups white bread flour

½ cup sugar

¼ cup warm milk

9 tbsp soft butter

2 tsp quick-acting dried yeast

3 tbsp melted butter

½ cup marzipan

¼ cup granulated sugar

¼ cup candied cherries

¼ cup flaked almonds

What you do

1 Put about ¾ of the **grated** peel, **candied** peel, fruit, and nutmeg in a saucepan. Add enough orange juice to cover them. Add a little lemon juice.

2 **Simmer** these ingredients together for about 10 minutes, until the liquid is **absorbed**. Let the mixture **cool**.

3 To make the **dough**, mix the flour, sugar, milk, soft butter, and **yeast** together with a ½ cup (120 ml) of warm water. **Knead** for 10 minutes on a floured board.

4 Put the dough in a bowl and **cover** it with plastic wrap. Put it in a warm place to **rise**, until it has doubled in size. This will take about 30 minutes.

5 Put the dough back on the board and **punch it down** before kneading the cooled fruit into it.

6 Divide the dough in half, and roll it into two rectangles. Brush each one with melted butter.

7 Cut the marzipan in half and roll each piece into a hotdog shape, the same width as the dough. Place a piece of marzipan on top of each piece of dough, then fold one side of each loaf over the other to enclose it. Press down on the tops of the loaves with a rolling pin to make sure that the dough is firmly stuck together.

8 Let the loaves rise again for about 30 minutes. **Preheat** the oven to 375°F (190°C). Then **bake** for about 35 minutes, until golden brown.

9 While the stollen are baking, **dissolve** the granulated sugar in 2 tbsp of **boiling** water to make a **glaze**. While they are still hot, paint the loaves with the glaze and **sprinkle** the candied cherries and flaked almonds over them for decoration.

Winter Fruit Salad (USA)

Dried fruits are very nutritious. They are available all year and keep for a long time. They are high in fiber and complex carbohydrates and contain many important vitamins and minerals needed for good health.

What you need

3 cups water

7 cups ready-to-eat dried fruits, such as prunes, pears, apricots, figs, and cranberries

1 tbsp clear honey

1 tsp vanilla extract

1 Earl Grey tea bag

Juice of 1 lemon

4 tbsp mascarpone cheese

What you do

 Fill a large saucepan with 3 cups (700 ml) of cold water and add the fruit, honey, and vanilla **extract**.

2 Place the saucepan over medium to high heat and bring the mixture to a **boil**.

3 Lower the heat, stir the mixture well, and **simmer** until it is slightly **syrupy** (about 10 minutes).

4 Take the pan off the heat and stir in the tea bag.

5 Leave the tea bag to infuse for 10 minutes, then discard it.

6 Pour the fruits and liquid into a heat-proof glass or plastic bowl and add the lemon juice.

7 Stir the mixture and leave it to **cool**.

8 **Cover** the bowl and chill the mixture until it is ready to serve.

9 Serve the fruit salad with the mascarpone cheese.

Amaretti (Italy)

These almond-flavored cookies are traditionally made in the south of Italy, where almonds are one of the most important crops.

What You need

2 cups ground almonds
½ cup granulated sugar
2 eggs
1 tsp almond extract

What You do

1 Mix the almonds and sugar together.

2 Separate the egg yolks from the whites. You can do this by breaking each egg, one at a time, into a bowl, and then using a spoon to carefully lift out the yolks.

3 **Whisk** the egg whites until they are stiff.

4 Mix the egg whites and the almond **extract** together with the almond and sugar mixture.

5 Line a baking sheet with **parchment paper**.

6 Spoon the mixture onto the sheet, using only half a teaspoon of mixture for each cookie.

7 Leave the cookies at room temperature for two hours. In this time they will dry out a little, and this will make the finished cookies crisper.

8 **Preheat** the oven to 350°F (180°C).

Ready to eat: 3 hours (including 2 hours for the cookies to dry). Difficulty: *.
Makes 30 cookies.

 **9** **Bake** the amaretti for about 15 minutes, or until they are light golden in color.

10 Allow the cookies to **cool** thoroughly before serving.

PRETTY PRESENTS

Amaretti make a wonderful Christmas present.
Wait until they are cool, and then wrap each
cookie up in pretty paper, before packing them
into a decorated tin or box.

Christmas Bread (Chile)

This bread is traditionally eaten on Christmas Eve, at a meal that brings the pre-Christmas **fast** to an end. It is very similar to Christmas breads and cakes that are eaten in Europe. This is because so many people from southern Europe settled in Chile and other South American countries in the past.

what you need

8 tbsp butter
½ cup granulated sugar
2 eggs
2 cups self-rising flour
½ cup milk
1 tsp baking powder
½ cup **candied** cherries
½ cup raisins
1/3 cup **chopped** almonds
½ cup mixed candied peel
Grated peel of 1 lemon

what you do

1. **Preheat** the oven to 300°F (150°C).

2. **Beat** the butter and the sugar together with a wooden spoon until they are light and fluffy.

3. Break the eggs into the bowl one by one and mix well. Add the flour and mix gently.

4. **Fold** in the remaining ingredients and mix well.

5. Spoon into a round, **greased**, 8-in. (20-cm) cake pan with a loose base.

6 **Bake** the bread in the oven for 1 hour 30 minutes. It is cooked when you can push a knife into its center and it comes out clean.

7 Allow the bread to **cool** for a couple of minutes and remove from the pan.

8 Cool completely and serve in slices. Christmas bread is especially tasty with butter spread over it.

Turrón (Spain)

Turrón is a special Christmas sweet from Spain. It is eaten at the end of a big family meal on Christmas Eve. The meal starts late—around 9 p.m.—and often includes seafood, meat, and fish. The turrón is served last, with the coffee.

What you need

- 4 eggs
- 4 cups finely chopped, **toasted** almonds
- ½ cup honey
- 1 cup granulated sugar
- A pinch of cinnamon
- Rice paper

What you do

1 Separate the egg yolks from the whites. You can do this by breaking each egg, one at a time, into a bowl, and then using a spoon to carefully lift out the yolks.

2 **Beat** the egg whites until they are stiff.

3 Mix in the almonds to make a **paste**.

4 Put the honey into a pan large enough to hold at least 8½ cups (2 liters) and heat very gently until it is runny. Honey gets very hot, so be careful not to splash yourself.

5 Add the sugar and continue to heat until it has melted into the honey. Now allow the mixture to **boil** gently. Be very careful, as boiling sugar is very hot. Be sure to have an adult to help you.

6 Add the paste of nuts and eggs to the honey mixture and stir without stopping over low heat for 10 minutes.

7 Line a large, shallow dish or cover a plastic **chopping** board with rice paper and pour the mixture on top. Use a heatproof spatula to spread it out in a thin layer.

8 Allow the mixture to **cool**. **Sprinkle** it with cinnamon.

9 After about 12 hours, when the turrón has set, break it into small pieces and serve.

RICE PAPER
Rice paper is a kind of paper that you can eat. Used in many sweet recipes, it is made from plant fiber.

Christmas Pudding Ice Cream (Australia)

Christmas comes in the middle of the Australian summer. Although some people have the traditional roast turkey, many others prefer a Christmas picnic, or a barbecue followed by ice cream or fruit salad. This is an Australian recipe for a refreshing Christmas pudding ice cream!

What you need

2 cups vanilla ice cream
½ cup ready-mixed
    dried fruit
½ **grated** apple
½ tsp cinnamon
½ tsp nutmeg
½ tsp ginger
1 tsp molasses
4 **candied** cherries,
    chopped
Squeeze of lemon juice
½ cup orange juice
A handful of chopped,
    toasted hazelnuts

What you do

1 Keep the ice cream in the freezer.

2 Put everything except the nuts and the ice cream into a small, nonstick saucepan. The orange juice should just cover the fruit.

3 Bring the mixture gently to a **boil**, stirring all the time, and cook until the liquid is **absorbed** and the fruit is plump. This should take about 10 minutes.

4 Put the mixture into a small bowl, **cover** it with plastic wrap, and put it in the refrigerator overnight.

5 Put a 4-cup (1-liter) bowl in the freezer, also overnight. The next morning, take the ice cream and the bowl out of the freezer; scoop the ice cream out of its container and into the bowl.

6 Using a fork, quickly stir the fruit mixture into the ice cream. You may have to wait a few minutes until the ice cream is soft enough to mix, but do not let it become runny. You should still have lumps of ice cream mixed with the fruit.

7 Serve the ice cream at once, scooping it out into bowls and decorating with a topping of **chopped** nuts.

Spiced Grape Juice (Germany)

In Germany there are open-air markets at Christmastime, where all sorts of good things are sold for the festive season. A spicy, hot wine drink called *Glühwein* is sold to help keep out the cold. This alcohol-free version of the drink uses grape juice instead of wine.

What you need

1 **unwaxed** orange
1 tsp cloves
½ unwaxed lemon
1-liter carton of
    unsweetened
    red grape juice
¼ cup honey
2 cinnamon sticks

What you do

1 Cut the orange in half, and then push the cloves into the skin of one half.

2 **Slice** the other half of the orange and the lemon half very thinly.

3 Pour the grape juice into the pan. It must either be a nonstick pan or one with an enamel lining. If you use an unlined metal pan, it will ruin the taste of your spiced grape juice.

4 Add the orange with the cloves in it, and the orange and lemon slices.

5 Add the honey, using a non-metal spoon.

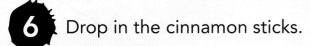 **6** Drop in the cinnamon sticks.

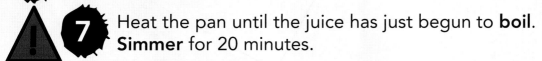 **7** Heat the pan until the juice has just begun to **boil**. **Simmer** for 20 minutes.

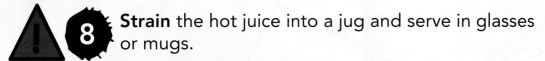 **8** **Strain** the hot juice into a jug and serve in glasses or mugs.

WAXED FRUIT

Some oranges and lemons are coated in wax before they are sold. This makes them look shinier and more attractive. If you have to use waxed oranges and lemons in this recipe, you may find that some froth forms on top of the juice as you simmer it. Use a non-metal spoon to skim this off.

Further Information

Here are some books and websites that will tell you about Christmas food and food for other festivals.

Books

Cornell, Kari A. *Holiday Cooking Around the World* (*Easy Menu Ethnic Cookbooks*). Minneapolis: Lerner, 2002.

Sindeldecker, Brittany, and Erica Sindeldecker. *Just for Kids Cookbook: Christmas at Home.* Uhrichsville, Ohio: Barbour, 2007.

Strand, Jessica, and Tammy Massman-Johnson. *Kids in the Holiday Kitchen: Making, Baking, Giving.* San Francisco: Chronicle, 2007.

Websites

www.apples4theteacher.com/holidays/christmas/kids-recipes

http://loveathome.com/archives/cwk07.htm

www.dreamsalivemagazine.com/christmas2003/columns/justforkids

http://recipes.kaboose.com/holidays/christmas-recipes/christmas-recipes.html

http://kidscooking.about.com/od/holidayandpartyfood/tp/Holiday-Recipes-for-Kids.htm

Healthy Eating

This diagram shows the types and proportion of food you should eat to stay healthy. Eat plenty of foods from the *grains* group and plenty from the *fruits* and *vegetables* groups. Eat some foods from the *milk* group and the *meat and beans* group. Foods from the *oils* group are not necessary for a healthy diet, so eat these in small amounts or only occasionally.

Healthy eating at Christmas

A great deal of the food that people eat at Christmas is not very healthy! Many traditional Christmas recipes are packed with sweet and fatty foods. Enjoy Christmastime—but remember to leave room for foods that are better for you!

↑ The MyPyramid food pyramid shows the proportion of food from each food group you should eat to achieve a healthy, balanced diet. This takes into account everything you eat, including snacks.

Glossary

absorb soak up

bake cook something in the oven

batter mixture of eggs, milk, and flour used for coating fried foods, or making pancakes

beat mix something together strongly, using a fork, spoon, or whisk

boil cook a liquid on the stove top. Boiling liquid bubbles and steams strongly.

broil cook by being exposed to direct heat

candied cooked in sugar. This is a way of making fruit keep for a long time.

chop cut something into pieces, using a knife

colander bowl-shaped container with holes in it, used for draining vegetables and straining

cool allow hot food to become cold. You should always allow food to cool before putting it in the refrigerator.

cover put a lid on a pan, or foil over a dish

dissolve mix something into a liquid until it disappears

dough soft mixture of flour and liquid that sticks together and can be shaped or rolled out. It is not too wet to handle, but it is not dry, either.

extract flavoring, such as vanilla or almond extract

fast to go without eating, ofted for religious reasons

fold mix ingredients together very slowly and carefully

fry cook something in oil in a pan

glaze liquid, such as a mixture of milk and egg, used to make tops of bread or buns glossy during baking

grate break something, such as cheese, into small pieces using a grater

grease rub fat over a surface to stop food from sticking to it

knead keep pressing and pushing dough with your hands so that it becomes very soft and stretchy

ovenproof will not crack in a hot oven

parchment paper kind of nonstick paper you can use to line baking sheets or cake pans, to stop things from sticking to them

paste thick mixture

peel remove the skin of a fruit or vegetable; or the skin itself

preheat turn on the oven or broiler in advance, so that it is hot when you are ready to use it

punch down kneading dough to get rid of big air bubbles. The air bubbles will be smaller when the dough rises for a second time.

rise grow bigger. Dough rises when the yeast in it starts to work.

season give extra flavor to food by adding salt or pepper

simmer cook a liquid on the stove top. Simmering liquid bubbles and steams gently.

slice cut something into thin, flat pieces

sprinkle scatter small pieces or drops onto something

strain pour a liquid through a sieve. If a liquid has bits of fruit or flavoring in it, straining can get rid of them.

syrup thick, sweet liquid made from sugar and water

thaw defrost something that has been in the freezer

toasted heated in a pan without any oil

translucent almost see-through. Onions become translucent when you fry them gently.

tropical coming from a warm area of earth near the Equator

unwaxed not treated with wax to make it look shiny

waxy potatoes varieties of potatoes with dense flesh that does not break up when cooked

whisk mix ingredients using a whisk

yeast substance used to make bread rise

Index